こどものためのピアノ曲集

ピアノの小径(こみち)

間宮芳生 作曲

The piano pieces for CHILDREN for small hands

KOMICHI for piano
—Pathway for piano—

composed by Michio Mamiya

©1985 by edition KAWAI, Tokyo, Japan.
International Copyright Secured, All Rights Reserved.

edition KAWAI

はじめに

　1985年夏から1986年夏にかけて，日記をつけるように書きためた，いろとりどりの，自由な姿の小品集です。そして世界のいろいろの地域の，さまざまな言葉を話すひとびとがうたい継いできた歌………踊り歌もあれば，まじない歌も，そして，子供の歌，大人の歌，子供も大人も一緒にうたう歌………などなどをもとにした曲も沢山入っています。

　それらの歌から聞こえてくる，世界のたくさんのひとびとの思いが，私の筆を進めてくれたので，それぞれは短いけれど，たっぷりと重い中味の音楽になったと思います。どの曲とも，練習しては忘れてゆくような具合でなく，長くつき合ってほしいと思います。

　技術的難度はみな似たりよったり。ですから，易しいのから順にという具合に並べることにはなりませんでした。そのかわり，最後の2曲の連弾曲を除く20曲を，一連の組曲として弾いて，うまく流れが出来るように考えました。とはいっても，順序を変えるのも，1曲または数曲を自由に選び出して弾くのも大歓迎です。

　指使いはなるべく書き入れるようにしました（あまり大きくない手のためを考えて）。ペダルの指示は，ほんの少しだけ書き込んであります。ペダルの使い方は，ピアノ演奏にとって，実はとても大切だけれど，楽譜に書き込んでもあまり役には立たないのです。耳を働かせて自分でいいふみ方を見つけ出すのが最上です。

間宮芳生

Preface

　These short pieces in various colors and shapes were composed, as a diary, from the summer of 1985 to the summer of 1986. They include many pieces derived from folksongs preserved by people who live in various parts of the world and speak different languages. The materials include dance songs, incantations, children's songs, adults' songs and songs sung by children and grownups together.

　The vividness of the thoughts and feelings of the people who sang those songs led me to compose these pieces. Therefore, they have turned out to be rather short but intensive. I hope that you will not forget them after practising, but keep company with them for a long time.

　In terms of technicality, they are more or less the same, so I have not arranged the pieces in order of technical difficulty. Instead, I have arranged them, except for the last two for four hands, to make a good flow as a suite composed of 20 pieces. However, the performer is welcome to play them in any different order, or choose a group of several or even one.

　I have indicated fingerings taking into consideration of children's rather small hands. I have given only a few marks for pedalling in the music. The ways of using pedals are very important for the piano performance. However, given instruction for pedalling in the music means very little. As for the pedalling, you should train yourself and find how to use them with exercising your own ears. It is only the way and the best way to get skilled in pedalling.

Michio Mamiya

もくじ		CONTENTS
1 スタディー I	4	Study I
2 スタディー II	6	Study II
3 スタディー III	8	Study III
4 オルゴール	10	Music Box
5 ロシアのうた	12	A Russian Song
6 ダンス	14	Dance
7 尺とり虫のインヴェンション	16	Inchworm's Invention
8 少年のヨーイク	18	Boy's Joiku
9 少女のヨーイク	20	Girl's Joiku
10 つむじかぜ	22	Whirlwind
11 3段とび変奏	24	Triple Jump Variations
12 夕ぐれのうた	26	Dusk
13 河のほとりで	28	On the Bank of the River
14 さびしいけれど，私は泣かない	30	I don't cry, lonely as I am
15 ピョートル	32	Peter
16 アシル	34	Achille
17 バルカンのうた	36	A Balkan Tune
18 黒と白と	38	Black and White
19 ふなうた	40	Barcarolle
20 ブンブン	43	Bun-bun
21 ハーディーガーディ（連弾）	46	(four hands) Hurdy-gurdy
22 オスティナート（連弾）	50	(four hands) Ostinato

表紙装幀・カット／佐野 洋子

1
スタディー I
Study I

間宮芳生 作曲
Michio Mamiya

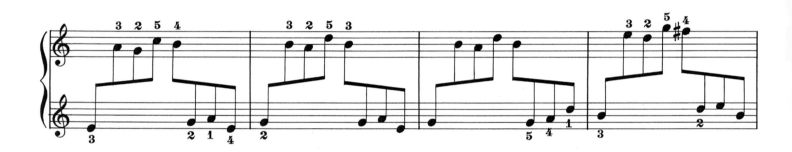

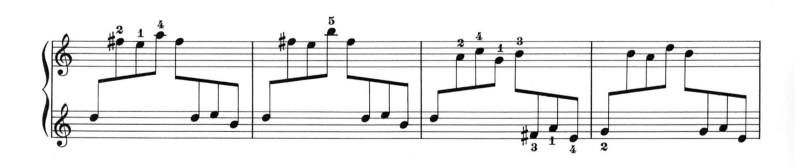

両方の手の協力（合作）で弾く一本のメロディー。スラー，スタッカート，フレーズなどの指示は一切しなかった。
レガートで，スタッカートで，その両方の組合せで，それから，いろいろなフレーズの切り方で試してほしい。

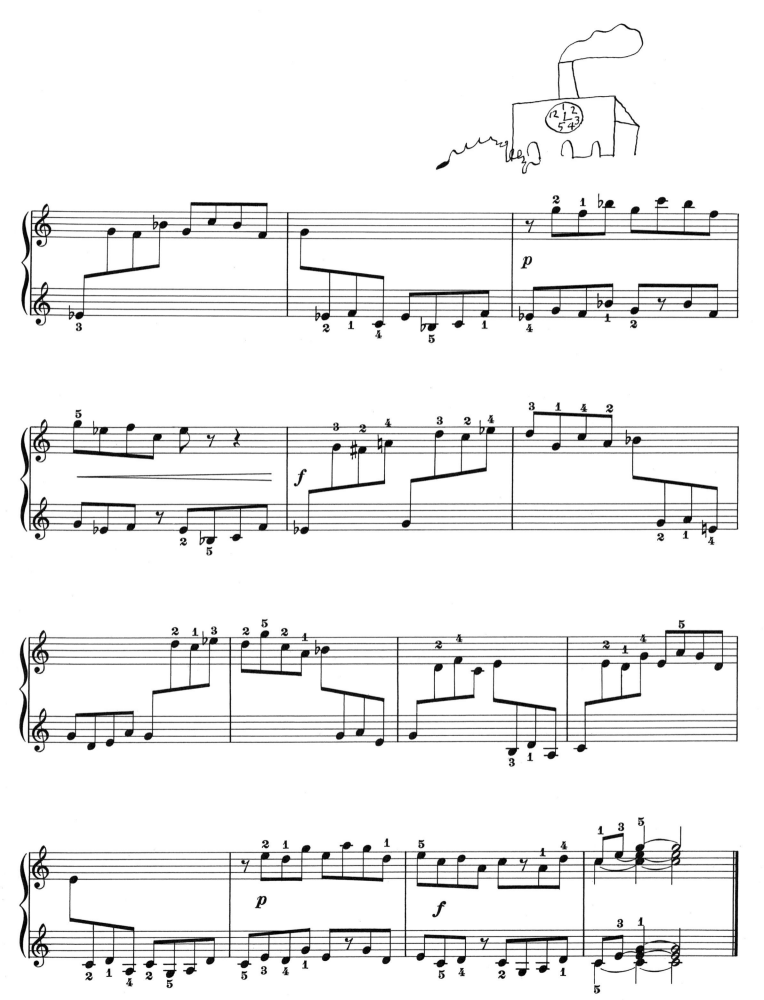

A melody line played by joint work of the two hands. No denotation such as for slur, staccato and phrasing is given in the music. Try to play in various manners; in legato, staccato, in the combination of both and at various phrasings.

スタディー II
Study II

間宮芳生 作曲
Michio Mamiya

スタディー 1 の変奏。

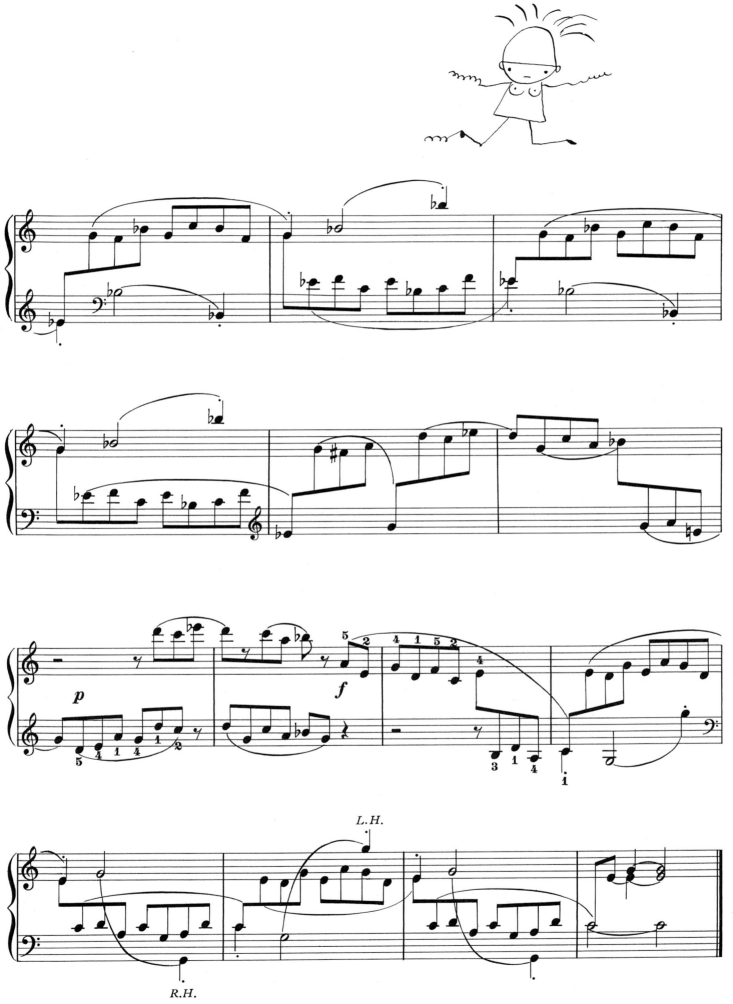

A variant of 'Study I'.

3
スタディー III
Study III

間宮芳生 作曲
Michio Mamiya

スタディーIのもうひとつの変奏。メロディーをオクターブのユニゾンで弾く。片手ずつ，あちらこちら音が抜いてある。それを気づかれないように弾くのも，反対に，うんと強調して弾くのも面白いだろう。スタディーIと同様に，スタッカート，レガート，などいろいろな弾き方を試してほしい。

Another variant of 'Study I' with an octave unison of the melody line. Some notes are omitted for one hand at a time. Try two ways of playing with and without emphasis of these blanks. Like 'Study I', various manners of phrasing and playing in staccato, legato etc., should also be tried.

Express the excitement you would have when you first open and listen to a music box which you had always wanted to have. The ending part should be played slower and slower in tempo, almost stopping, like a music box runs down.

An old Russian folksong, not so known. "A Cossack soldier went to a faraway country and died. A girl, longing for his return innocently, prays towards the northern sky." Express a sadness of the song, but do not it with too much feeling. Make a clear alternation of staccato and legato in the second half of the piece.

Two Finnish folk melodies are combined together in this piece. Play in flowing steps for the first half, and play the staccato with tenths for the left hand in the second half like hopping. Melody for the right hand should sound like the violin.

Phrases with double notes should be played in legato but in solid sounds. Fingers walk on the keys with steady strides. Inchworm's strides might give you a good suggestion.

ヨーイクは，スカンジナビアの北極圏，ラップランドに住むサーミ族の民謡。もともとまじない歌で，今は村の人々ひとりひとりのテーマ・メロディーとして歌われる。大てい言葉ぬきでうたうが，聞く人はそれが誰のテーマ・メロディーか，すぐわかるのだ。

Joiku is the folksong handed down by Saame people who live in Lapland, the Arctic area of the Scandinavian countries. Joiku was originally magical song, but now it is sung as the theme melody of each village dweller. They are mostly sung without words. By listening to the singing of each joiku without words, the village people can tell who it belongs to.

9
少女のヨーイク
Girl's Joiku

間宮芳生 作曲
Michio Mamiya

左手は伴奏ではない。ギクシャクと上り下りの多い旋律が，ヨーイクのひとつの特徴だ。ときどきは1オクターブより広い跳躍もある。左右の手をつなげたそのギクシャクが，ひとりの声でうたっているように聞こえなければならない。

The left hand is not an accompaniment. One of the characteristics of joiku is the zigzags of their melody lines with wide intervals, sometimes wider than an octave. The zigzags played by passing over between the two hands should sound like single singing voice.

くどうなおこの詩による自作の童謡「ぼくはかぜのこ」のメロディーによる。つむじかぜが、くるくる落葉を巻くようなスピード感をもって弾くこと。中間部は、これもヨーイクのメロディー。

Based on a children's song "I am a wind boy", written by Naoko Kudo and composed by myself. Play with speed of whirlwind, rolling up the fallen leaves. The middle section is derived from one of the joiku tunes.

11
3段とび変奏
Triple Jump Variations

間宮芳生 作曲
Michio Mamiya

テーマと二つの変奏。日本の民謡にもよくある四度音程が重なって3段とびをしているようなメロディーだ。テーマは大らかに，第1の変奏は半音階進行をデリケートに，第2の変奏は，長いレガートの大きな山型になるよう気を配ろう。

Theme and two variations. The melody, suggestive of triple jump, is made of piles of fourths which are often found in Japanese folksongs. Play the theme grandly, and the chromatic progression in the first variation with delicacy. Pay attention to play the second variation in legato to make two big mountain shapes of the melody.

12
夕ぐれのうた
Dusk

間宮芳生 作曲
Michio Mamiya

夕もやに包まれた，暖かい空気をはだに感じるように。やわらかな和音と，パンフルートを思い出すような透明な
メロディーの流れにしよう。とくに，ペダルをうまく使うことが必要。

As if to sense the warm air in the hazy evening, play the chords with tenderness. The flows of clear melody should sound like the pan-pipe. Skillful and sensitive use of pedals is also expected.

アフリカからアメリカへ運ばれた黒人どれいの民謡。題の「河のほとり」にとくべつのいわれはない。"アメリカ南部の農場,……ミシシッピー河……その河に向って神の加護をいのる声" このメロディーをそう聞きとって私がつけた題だ。身にしみるようなこのメロディーから聞こえる祈りの気持をあらわそう。

A folksong of the black slave taken to America from Africa. There is no special ground for its titling, except I heard in the melody the images of ... "A big farm in the south of America ... the Mississippi River ... the singing voice by the black people towards the river praying to God for his blessing." Express the deep feeling of prayer which can be heard in this touching melody.

14
さびしいけれど，私は泣かない
I don't cry, lonely as I am

間宮芳生 作曲
Michio Mamiya

フィンランドの古い民謡。拍子のわくにしばられず，自由な呼吸で弾くのがいい。左手の平行に動く和音をペダルでやわらかくつなげること。

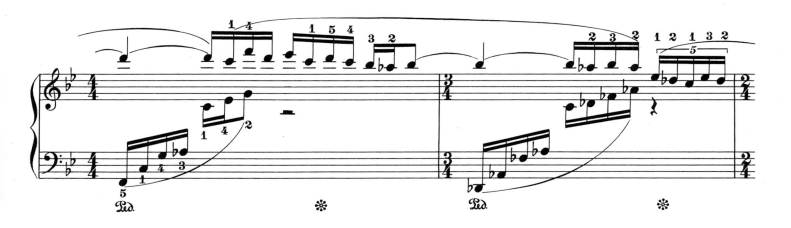

An old Finnish folksong. Not limitted by meter, play at free expression with tempo rubato. Play the chords in parallel progression for the left hand in legato by sensitive use of the right pedal.

15 ピョートル
Peter

間宮芳生 作曲
Michio Mamiya

ピョートルは,「くるみ割り人形」や「白鳥の湖」を作曲した,ロシアの作曲家,チャイコフスキーのファーストネーム。はずむスタッカートは,とても美しい水玉模様のような木管楽器のひびきだ。

Peter is the first name of Tschaikowsky, a Russian composer who composed "the Nutcracker" and "the Swan Lake". Springing staccato should sound like the woodwind instruments reminding us of the beautiful polka dots.

16
アシル
Achille

間宮芳生 作曲
Michio Mamiya

フランス印象派の作曲家，クロード・ドビュッシーのミドル・ネーム。このはじまりのモティーフは，実は日本の民謡のメロディーだ。いつもペダルでくるんで，木もれ陽のやわらかいひびきのような音を。そしてドビュッシーの音楽をこれからぜひ沢山弾いてほしい。

Achille is the middle name of Debussy, a French impressionist composer. The motif at the beginning of the piece came from a Japanese folksong. By use of two pedals, make the sounds as tender as sunbeams shining through foliage. And I hope you will play a lot of Debussy's music hereafter.

17 バルカンのうた
A Balkan Tune

間宮芳生 作曲
Michio Mamiya

Moderato ♩≒102 (♩≒68) うねって、しかしテンポは保って

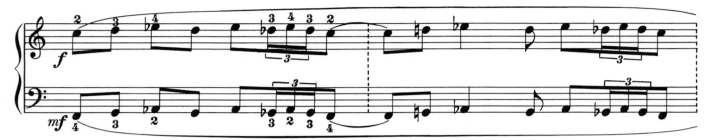

注）臨時記号は，点線で区切られた範囲内で有効です。

東洋と西洋の間のちょうど廊下みたいなバルカン半島だから，アラビヤ音楽の宝がどっさり入って来ていて，ブルガリヤにも，こういうアラビヤ風の不規則なリズムの息の長いメロディーが沢山ある。

The Balkan Peninsular has been enriched by the fortunes of the Arabian music, because it lies like a corridor between the East and the West. Therefore, in the Bulgarian folk music, for example, one finds a lot of the Arabesque tunes of long melody with irregular rhythm.

The title means, of course, the black keys and the white keys of the piano. You may play some notes with the edge of your fists. Try to jump around on the keyboard in spirits.

19
ふなうた
Barcarolle

間宮芳生 作曲
Michio Mamiya

右手のメロディーをなだらかに弾くには，いい指使いが必要。指示した指使いは一例で，外のも工夫してほしい。
左手の伴奏形は，強さの変化によく気を配って，うたを支えることが大切だ。

Good fingering is necessary to play the melody smoothly with the right hand. The fingering indicated in the music is one example, and you may try to find another. To support the melody give your attention to variation of dynamics for accompanying left hand.

Bun-bun is an Indonesian marimba made of bamboo. The original form of the piece has been taken from the Ghanaian folk music, which has duple and triple time in a single bar.

21
ハーディーガーディー
Hurdy-gurdy

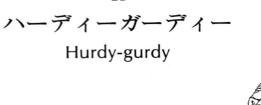

Secondo

間宮芳生 作曲
Michio Mamiya

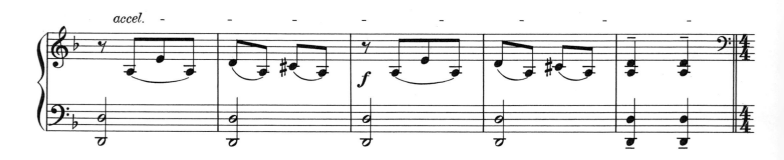

ハーディーガーディーは，手まわしハンドルを回すと音が出る楽器。音程は指で鍵盤をひいてつくるし，音はちょうどバイオリンの音。中世ヨーロッパで愛用された民俗楽器だ。曲の中味は，ちょっとハンガリーのジプシー音楽風だ。テンポの変わり方を上手にやると楽しさが倍増するだろう。

Hurdy-gurdy is a musical instrument, in which the sound is produced by turnning a crank. Fingers pushing the key-board make the pitches, and sound is just like the violin. Hurdy-gurdy was very popular as a folk instrument in the medieval Europe. The piece has a characteristic somewhat similar to the Gypsy music of Hungary. If you can carefully manipulate the variation in tempo you will find the piece very attractive.

48

Secondo

Allegro non troppo ♩=128

Poco andante

Allegro non troppo

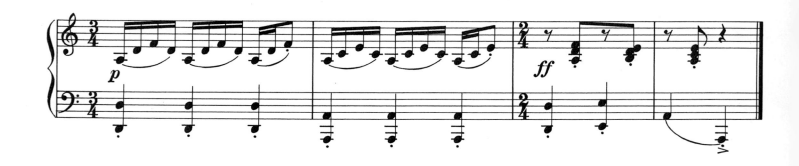

22 オスティナート
Ostinato

Secondo

間宮芳生 作曲
Michio Mamiya

オスティナートは，しつこくくり返されるメロディー（又は伴奏型）のこと。しかし単なるくり返しでなく，第1ピアノのパートに反応して伴奏型の表情がゆれて変って弾かれると，一層生き生きするだろう。モデラートからの第2ピアノの和音の表情も大切に。

Ostinato is a melody or accompanying form which is repeated persistently. However, if the accompanying part responds vividly to the primo, the performance will have a bright nature. Play the chords for the second piano from Moderato with much expression.

Secondo

作曲者のプロフィール

- 1929 年　北海道旭川市に生れる。
- 1933 年　父を師としてピアノを学ぶ。
- 1948 年　東京音楽学校（現・東京芸術大学）作曲科に入学、池内友次郎に師事。
- 1952 年　同学校卒業。
  毎日音楽賞受賞（1959 年）をはじめ、毎日芸術賞、尾高賞、福山賞、ザルツブルグテレビオペラ賞金賞等多くの賞を受賞。

これまでに、東京芸術大学講師（1972～91）、桐朋学園大学講師、後同大学特任教授（1980～2005）、静岡音楽館芸術監督（1995～2005）等を歴任。

- 主要作品　オペラ「昔噺人買太郎兵衛」・「ニホンザル・スキトオリメ」・「鳴神」・「ポポイ」、合唱のためのコンポジション第 1 番～第 17 番、日本民謡集（独唱とピアノのための）全 27 曲、弦楽四重奏曲第 1 番・第 2 番・第 3 番、オーケストラのための二つのタブロー'65、ピアノ協奏曲第 2 番、ヴァイオリン協奏曲第 1 番・第 2 番、チェロ協奏曲、オーケストラのためのタブロー'85。
- 著　書　「野のうた氷の音楽」「現代音楽の冒険」

Biographical Sketch

- 1929; born in Asahikawa, Hokkaido.
- 1933; bigan his musical training with his father.
- 1948; entered the Academy of Music, Tokyo (now the National University of Fine Arts and Music of Tokyo), majored in composition with Prof. Tomojiro Ikenouchi.
- 1952; graduated from the Academy.
  received the Mainichi Music Prize.(1959)
  Since then, he won many prizes for his compositions including the Mainichi Art Prize, the Odaka Prizes, the Fukuyama Music Prize, and Grand Prix of the Salzburg Television Opera Prize.
  He tought as a lecturer at the Tokyo National University of Fine Arts and Music (1972-91), as a lecturer, later as a professor at the Toho-gakuen School of Music (1980-2005) and worked as the Artistic Director of the Concert Hall Shizuoka (1995-2005).
- works (selective list of compositions)
  operas : Mukashibanashi "Hitokai Tarobei" (Tale of Tarobei, the Slave Dealer) / Nihonzaru Sukitoorime (Clairvoyant Monkey Painter) / Narukami (The Thunder Father) / Popoi.
  Compositions for Chorus Nos. 1-17; Japanese Folksong Collection (27 pieces for voice with piano accompaniment); String Quartets Nos. 1,2,3; Deux Tableaux pour Orchestre '65; piano Concerto No.2; Violin Concertos Nos. 1,2; Cello Concerto; Tableau pour Orchestre '85.
- literary work
  "No-no Uta, Koori-no ongaku" (Wild song and music of ice), "Gendai Ongaku-no Boken" (Adventure of Contemporary Music)

■ CDのご案内
世界のこどもたちへ「間宮芳生・ピアノの部屋」（ALCD-83）
演奏：中嶋 香（ピアノ）
にほんのこども 44 曲／ピアノの小径 全 22 曲収録
お問い合わせ：コジマ録音（Tel.03-5397-7311）

携帯サイトはこちら▶

出版情報＆ショッピング　**カワイ出版ONLINE**　http://editionkawai.jp

こどものためのピアノ曲集
ピアノの小径

発行日● 1987 年 2 月 1 日　第 1 刷発行	作　曲●間宮芳生	
2025 年 6 月 1 日　第 10 刷発行	発行所●カワイ出版（株式会社 全音楽譜出版社 カワイ出版部）	
	〒161-0034　東京都新宿区上落合 2-13-3	
	TEL.03-3227-6286　FAX.03-3227-6296	
	楽譜浄書●ミタニガクフ	
	写植●創美写植	
表紙装幀・カット●佐野洋子	印刷／製本●平河工業社	

© 1985 by edition KAWAI. Assigned 2017 to Zen-On Music Co., Ltd.

本書よりの転載はお断りします。
落丁・乱丁本はお取り替え致します。
本書のデザインや仕様は予告なく変更される場合がございます。

ISBN978-4-7609-0518-8